The Baghdad Blues

Harbor Mountain Press acknowledges the support of
Pentangle Council on the Arts (Woodstock, Vermont)
for this and other literary projects.

Poems in this volume were first published in
Across Borders, Banipal, and elsewhere.
Many thanks to the editors and publishers who have
published Sinan Antoon's work.

First printing 2007

ISBN 0-9786009-4-0

Series Editor:
Peter Money

Cover illustration:
Mohammed Al Shammarey
www.shammarey.com

Production editing:
Barbara Jones

Harbor Mountain Press
Brownsville, Vermont
0 5 0 3 7

www.harbormountainpress.com

The Baghdad Blues

Sinan Antoon

Harbor Mountain Press
Brownsville, Vermont

Contents

Wars I

A Prism; Wet With Wars

this is the chapter of
devastation
this is our oasis
an angle where wars intersect
tyrants accumulate around our eyes
in the shackle's verandah
there is enough space for applause
let us applaud

another evening climbs
the city's candles
technological hoofs crush the night
people are being slaughtered across short waves
but the radio vomits raw statements
and urges us to
applaud

with a skeleton of a burning umbrella
we receive this rain
a god sleeps on our flag
but the horizon is prophetless
maybe they will come if we
applaud
let us applaud

we will baptize our infants with smoke
plough their tongues
with flagrant war songs
or UN resolutions
teach them the bray of slogans
and leave them beside burning nipples
in an imminent wreckage
and applaud

before we weave an autumn for tyrants
we must cross this galaxy of barbed wires
and keep on repeating
HAPPY NEW WAR!

Baghdad, March 1991

Wars II

When I was torn by war

I took a brush
Immersed in death
And drew a window
On war's wall
I opened it
Searching
For something
But
I saw another war
And a mother
Weaving a shroud
For the dead man
Still in her womb

Baghdad, 1990

A Prisoner's Song

(for the POWs of the Iraq-Iran war 1980-1988 . . . on both sides)

from the distant fog
after communiqués had withered
and canons stopped spitting
he returned
soaked with the "there"
his silence an umbrella
under our ululation
he passed by us
through us
to his old room
the lute was still there
its strings in their wooden exile
yearned for his rainy fingers
but he never touched it
what language could explain
that eight years
had gnawed
ten fingers

Baghdad, April 1990

The Milky Way

your nipple
is a rounded decade
of strawberries
my tongue
a tribe
of motherless fingers
climbing
the marble dome
of an atheist temple
angels wail for asylum
I swim in a fountain
of undeciphered languages
but
in the morning
your bra
strangles
my metaphors

1989

To an Iraqi infant

do you know
that your mother's nipples
are dry bones?
that her breasts
are bursting
with depleted uranium?

do you know
that the womb's window
overlooks
a confiscated land?

do you know
that your tomorrow
has no tomorrow?
that your blood
is the ink
of new maps?

do you know
that your mother is weaving
the slowness of her moments
into an elegy?

And she is already
mourning you?
don't be shy!
your funeral is over
the tears are dry
everyone's gone

come forward!
it's only a short way
don't be late
your grave is looking
at its watch!

don't be afraid!
We'll arrange your bones
which ever way you want
and leave your skull
like a flower
on top

come forward!
your many friends await
there are more
every day
. . .
your ghosts
will play together

come on!

New York, December 2002

Delving

The sea is a lexicon
of blueness
assiduously read
by the sun
your body, too
is a lexicon
of my desires
its first letter
will take a lifetime!

Beirut, April, 2003

Phantasmagoria I

blue rain

addressing a silent orchestra
in a distant morning
the maestro cannot read
the foggy lines
butterflies bloom
from your vocal cords
and colonize my memory

Baghdad, 1989

Phantasmagoria II

your lips
are a pink butterfly
flying
from one word
to another
i run after them
in gardens
of silence

Cairo, June, 2003

Vista

the sea rests its head
on the horizon's pillow
and takes a siesta
I can hear its blueness
breathing
whenever the sun's fingertips
kiss its skin
the sky gets jealous

Beirut, April, 2003

Insomnia

1.

insomnia's fingers leaf
through my minutes
my night is a desert
and sleep
is roaming nomads
I see them

A   p   p   r   o   a   c   h   i   n   g
 A   p   p   r   o   a   c   h   i   n   g
  A   p   p   r   o   a   c   h   i   n   g
   A p p r o a c h i n g
    A p p r o a c h i n g
     A p p r o a c h i n g
      A p p r o a c h i n g

Only to declare
themselves
the letters of a mirage

2.

sleeplessness
is my pillow
a pillow hiding
thousands of birds
whose quills crowd my head
each one inscribing
my insomnia
the night is ink

3

my eyelids
are butterflies
darkness
is their meadow

Cairo, June, 2003

Sifting

my eyes
are two sieves
sifting
in piles of others
for you

Cairo, August 2003

Wrinkles; on the wind's forehead

1

the wind is a blind mother
stumbling
over the corpses
no shrouds
save the clouds
but the dogs
are much faster

2

the moon is a graveyard
for light
the stars women
wailing

3

the wind was tired
from carrying the coffins
and leaned
against a palm tree
A satellite inquired:
Whereto now?
the silence
in the wind's cane murmured:
"Baghdad"
and the palm tree caught fire

4

the soldier's fingers scrape
and scrabble
like question marks
or sickles
they search the womb
of the wind
for weapons
. . .
nothing but smoke
and depleted uranium

5

how narrow is this strait
which sleeps
between two wars
but I must cross it

6

My heart is a stork
perched on a distant dome
in Baghdad
it's nest made of bones
its sky
of death

7

This is not the first time
myths wash their face
with our blood
(t)here they are
looking in horizon's mirror
as they don our bones

8

war salivates
tyrants and historians pant
a wrinkle smiles
on the face of a child
who will play
during a break
between wars

9

The Euphrates
is a long procession
Cities pat its shoulders
as palm trees weep

10

The child plays
in time's garden
but war calls upon her
from inside:
come on in!

11

The grave is a mirror
into which the child looks
and dreams:
when will I grow up
and be like my father
. . .
dead

12

the Tigris and Euphrates
are two strings
in death's lute
and we are songs
or fingers strumming

13

For two and a half wars
I've been here
in this room
whose window is a grave
that I'm afraid of opening
there is a mirror on the wall
when I stand before it
naked
my bones laugh
and I hear death's fingers
tickling the door

14

I place my ear
on the belly of this moment
I hear wailing
I put it on another moment:
– the same!

Cairo, May-June, 2003

Just another evening (in black and you)

1

your voice floats
on the evening's water
like a sleepy narcissus
and I am a shore
thinking of drowning

2

every touch
is a white envelope
hiding tens of letters
also white
letters penned by your nudity
about itself

3

your shirt
is an open envelope
your breasts
two letters
always
about to arrive

4

even the night's fingers
whisper
as they think
of undressing you

A Sip

when your fingers embrace
the glass's waist
a smile awakens
in the dream of a man
asleep in a distant night

it's been a long day
he's blown his soul
into many a glass

the jasmine wind in your wrist
caresses his pillow
when your lip touches the tip of the glass
thousands of wild horses begin to rush
in his veins
their whinniying blends
with the wine raining from above
the nude women on horsebacks
declare him a hedonistic prophet

you put the glass back on the table
he wakes up
looks at his watch–
in an hour
he will enter a new day
like a long tunnel

Cairo, August 2003

String

1

the player's fingers climb
the musical scales
and carry me
to the clouds
then descend
followed by God
who weeps
and apologizes for everything

2

the strings of the lute
pull my soul
from the well of silence
fill my heart
with the sea's blueness
storm my branches
pluck me
scattering me far away
on an island
outside time
inside my heart

3

this umbilical cord
extends from my heart
to the banks of the Euphrates
I sever it every morning
but, at night,
nostalgia
mends it

4

a thread
that rains from the needle's eye
in a night
whose blackness
tires the candles
as they count its minutes
a thread used by a mother
to mend a shirt
that still remembers the scent
of the prisoner
she's been waiting for
for eleven autumns
. . .
a shirt
no one will ever wear

5

a shelf
in the heart's archives
where postponed deaths
are stacked
next to rumors
about happiness

6

the border line
across the provinces
of nostalgia
between a country
that never was
and a country
which will never be–
whenever it is pulled away
by imagination
there
history
brings it back
here

7

the sobbing of a man
as he clings to the thread
running from his fingers
towards a white kite
still soaring
in the skies of his childhood
outside the cell
on his execution night

8

a silk thread
sighs
and thinks of eloping
from a black bra
. . .
it is fatigued
and does not want to stop
the two breasts
from kissing

9

an invisible ray
seizes my heart
the scent of a woman
who would be passing by me
twenty years from now
had she not died
in the last war

10

the last line
in a manuscript
whose burning
has been delayed
eight centuries

11

the migration route
taken by a rare bird
in its last season
before extinction

12

the shadow of the last palm tree
in a burning orchard
as its fronds comb
the wind's hair
and it is consoled
by the sun

13

perhaps
the string is merely
a string
consoling the trees
crucified in the body of the lute
or is it just yearning
for another string
crucified
in a distant lute

Cairo, April-June 2003

Clouds
(For J)

all the clouds
of the world
are waiting
in my body
you
are their
wind,
sky,
and earth

New York, November 2006

A Photograph

(Of An Iraqi Boy on the Front Page of the *New York Times*)

he sat
at the edge of the truck
(eight or nine years old?)
surrounded by his family:
his father,
mother,
and five siblings
were asleep
his head was buried
in his hands
all the clouds of the world
were waiting
on the threshold of his eyes
the tall man wiped off the sweat
and started digging
the seventh grave

New York, September 2006

Absence

when you leave
the place withers
I gather the clouds
scattered by your lips
hang them on the walls
of my memory
and wait
for another day

SINAN ANTOON is a poet, novelist and translator. He studied English literature at Baghdad University before moving to the United States after the 1991 Gulf War. He did his graduate studies at Georgetown and Harvard where he received a Ph.D in Arabic literature. His poems and articles (in Arabic and English) have appeared in *an-Nahar, as-Safir, Masharef, al-Adab, The Nation, Middle East Report, al-Ahram Weekly, Banipal* and the *Journal of Palestine Studies*. He has published a collec*tion of poems Mawshur Muballal bil-Huroob (A Prism; Wet with Wars,* Mirit Books, Cairo) and a novel *I'jaam* (Beirut, 2004) (forthcoming in English from City Lights in 2007). His poems were anthologized in *Iraqi Poetry Today.* Antoon returned to Iraq in 2003 as a member of InCounter Productions to co-direct and co-produce a documentary entitled "About Baghdad" about the lives of Iraqis in a post-Saddam occupied Iraq. He is a member of Pen America, a contributing editor to *Banipal* and a member of the editorial committee of Middle East Report. He teaches Arabic culture at New York University.